M18 Hellcat Tank Destroyer

Written by David Doyle

Walk Around®

U.S.A.
40145397

19

7A-807-TD

C24

Squadron Signal®
Publications

Color Art by Don Greer
Line Art by Melinda Turnage

(Front Cover) An M18 Gun Motor Carriage of the 4th Armored Division, 3rd U.S. Army crosses the Moselle on a treadway bridge at Müden, Germany, in March 1945.

(Back Cover) An M18 crew uses their 76mm cannon and .50-caliber machine gun to control an intersection in Frambois, France, in September of 1944.

About the Walk Around® Series

The Walk Around® series is about the details of specific military equipment using color and black-and-white archival and photographs of in-service, preserved, and restored equipment. *Walk Around*® titles are devoted to aircraft and military vehicles. These are picture books focus on operational equipment, not one-off or experimental subjects.

Squadron/Signal Walk Around® books feature the best surviving and restored historic aircraft and vehicles. Inevitably, the requirements of preservation, restoration, exhibit, and continued use may affect these examples in some details of paint and equipment. Authors strive to highlight any feature that departs from original specifications.

 Proudly printed in the U.S.A.
Copyright 2012 Squadron/Signal Publications
1115 Crowley Drive, Carrollton, TX 75006-1312 U.S.A.
www.SquadronSignalPublications.com

Hardcover ISBN 978-0-89747-697-3
Softcover ISBN 978-0-89747-698-0

Military/Combat Photographs and Snapshots

If you have any photos of aircraft, armor, soldiers, or ships of any nation, particularly wartime snapshots, please share them with us and help make Squadron/Signal's books all the more interesting and complete in the future. Any photograph sent to us will be copied and returned. Electronic images are preferred. The donor will be fully credited for any photos used. Please send them to the address above.

(Title Page) With a top speed of 60 miles per hour, the M18 Hellcat – or Hell-Cat in the early terminology of M18 manufacturer Buick – was the fastest World War II armored fighting vehicle. Lightly armored, the 76mm Gun Motor Carriage (GMC) crews relied on the Hellcat's high speed, as well as its low profile, for protection when battling Axis foes. Specialized tank destroyer units equipped with the M18 and other specialized weapons formed the core of a flawed U.S. Army antitank strategy during the Second World War.

Dedication

To the brave men who formed America's Tank Destroyer Battalions during World War II, and who did their part to turn the tide of battle against the formidable Axis military forces. Whether crewmen or support troops, all gave some, and some gave all to secure victory for the Allies.

Introduction

The vehicle that came to be known as the M18 was the result of a convoluted development process that began in fall, 1941. At that time U.S. Army doctrine held that a force of dedicated tank destroyers would thwart enemy armored assaults. General Lesly McNair, head of Army Ground Forces, decreed that half of these antitank forces be towed weapons, contrary to the wishes of the head of the Tank Destroyer Center, Colonel A. D. Bruce, who advocated heavily armed, very fast, self-propelled tank destroyers. Development progressed through a series of vehicles – the 37mm Gun Motor Carriage T42; the 57mm Gun Motor Carriage T49; the 75mm Gun Motor Carriage T67; and finally in early 1943, the 76mm Gun Motor Carriage T70, which in March 1944 was standardized as the M18. Buick, the builder of the vehicles, dubbed it the Hellcat. The T70 entered production before testing of the six pilot models had been completed.

The ongoing testing of the pilots revealed deficiencies, which resulted in changes to the vehicle design after production had begun, as well as the decision to return vehicles serial number 684 and below to the factory for modification. The most significant modification made on these early vehicles was a change in transmission gear ratios. Ultimately, however, 650 of those vehicles returned to the factory were converted to M39 and T41E1 Armored Utility Vehicles. Despite initial plans to produce 8,986 M18s, the changing tide of the war, a shift in Army tank destroyer doctrine, and the growing inadequacy of the 76mm M1 gun against German tank armor resulted in production being limited to 2,507 examples. Despite these shortcomings, and its relatively swift obsolescence in U.S. service, the M18 continued as a front-line fighting vehicle for other nations for decades, even serving into the 1990s in Serbia-Yugoslavia.

Acknowledgments

Assembling a large collection of detailed photographs documenting a combat vehicle requires access to the vehicle, at a minimum for several hours, more often over several days. It has been a blessing and a privilege that not only have so many of these enthusiasts allowed me to crawl in, over, under, and through these vehicles – but also for them to be considered friends. Without their help, this book would not have been possible. The early M18 section of this book features a vehicle restored by Frank Buck, which is now in the collection of the Military History Institute, and an M18 owned by Fred Ropkey. A third early M18 is owned and restored by Brent Mullins. Brent also did the restoration work on the late M18 owned by Bill Bauer, which is shown in operation in the late M18 portion of the book. Also featured there is an M18 owned by Allan Cors and restored by Marc Sehring. The bulk of the photos in the late M18 section present an M18 owned and restored by Steve Preston, and extensively photographed by James Alexander and myself. Steve also answered endless questions about the M18. Surviving T70 pilot number 3, featured early in the book, belongs to the U.S. Army Ordnance Museum. Also invaluable to completing this project was the help of Tom Kailbourn, Joe DeMarco, Pierre-Olivier Buan, Jim Gilmore, and Steve Zaloga and most of all, my lovely wife Denise.

An M10 tank destroyer overshadows the T70, which has a markedly lower silhouette. Not apparent in photos is another advantage of the T70 – its high speed. (Joe Demarco)

The T70, as the early Hellcats were designated, while armed with a 76mm gun, utilized essentially the same hull design found on the T49. Unfortunately, time would show that an even larger cannon would have been desirable. (Patton Museum)

M18 Hellcat Tank Destroyer

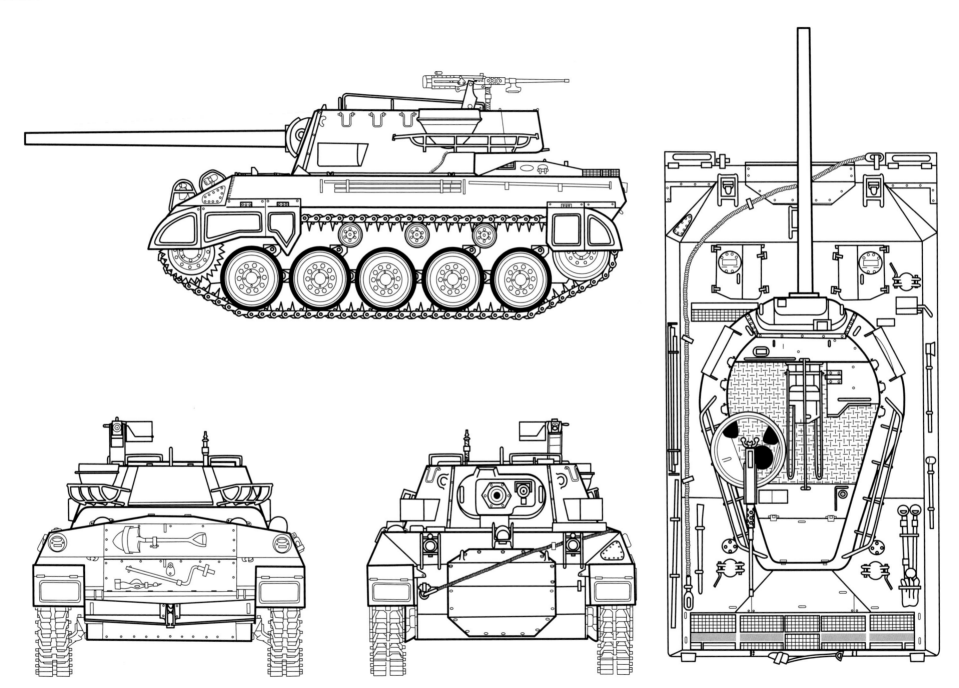

The T70 was the designation of the pilot vehicles that would be standardized as the 76mm GMC M18. In early 1943, the Buick Motor Division contracted to build six examples of the 76mm GMC T70, delivering all six vehicles to the Army by July of that year. The T70 had the Continental R-975-C1 radial engines mounted in the rear of the hull and the 900T Torqmatic transmission and the final drives in the front of the hull. At the heart of the T70 was the 76mm gun M1 – a more powerful antitank weapon than the 75mm gun M3 of the 75mm GMC T67, a prototype that was discontinued in favor of the T70. This example, the third T70, is in the collection of the U.S. Army Ordnance Museum. It has been redone markings not original to the vehicle, to represent an M18 76mm GMC, *Fearless Felix,* U.S. Army registration number 40145153.

At the front of the hull of the T70, from the level of the headlights on down, was a bolted-on door for accessing or removing the transmission. The transmission was mounted on tracks, and, to remove it, it was simply rolled forward out of the vehicle.

The driver's and co-driver's hatch doors on the earliest T70s were split laterally. The doors seen here, split from front to rear, were the type used on production M18s. On the gun shield, or mantlet, is the hinged, armored shield for the gunner's telescope.

The drive sprockets, located at the front of the hull, each have 31 teeth, with the tracks engaging between every second tooth. Two hydraulic double-acting shock absorbers are above the front road wheel, and one shock absorber is above the next wheel.

On top of the left side of the hull, aft of the driver's hatch, is a raised hood and grille for a ventilator, found on early M18s. It served as an air-outlet vent for the transmission and differential oil coolers. Later M18s had a flush-mounted air-outlet vent on the hull roof.

Above the rear of the hull of the T70, seen in the lower half of the photo, is the rear of the turret bustle, or overhang. To the immediate right of the star insignia is a holder for a shovel handle, while to the far left is a holder for the shovel's blade.

On the rear deck at the center of the photo are the right fuel tank cap cover and a fuel tank gauge cover. To the lower left is a bracket for stowing an M3 machine gun tripod. To the far left are air outlet grilles. The air inlet grille is below the turret bustle.

Further details of the rear of the T70 are exhibited, including the welded-on mounts for the tail light assemblies. Below the star is the bolted-on engine-access door. Like the transmission, the engine was mounted on tracks so it could be removed easily.

Projecting from each side of the turret is a rack of welded tubular construction for stowing bedrolls and equipment. To the lower left and the lower right are the left and right fuel tank cap covers. The rear of the turret has ½-inch armor.

At the bottom in this photo of the right side of the rear deck of the T70 is a clamp for securing the tripod for the vehicle's .50-caliber machine gun, which could be removed from its turret mount and mounted on the tripod for firing away from the vehicle.

On the top of the hull to the right front of the turret is a hood-type holder for two handles for actuating the fixed fire-extinguishing system. To the right are the vent (the hooded grille) and exhaust (the tube welded to the side of the hull) for the auxiliary generator.

An open bin welded to the right side of the turret was for stowing a collapsible driver's hood, which was mounted over the driver's hatch during bad weather. The U-shaped swiveling brackets near the top of the turret supported a canvas cover over the turret.

In a view of the front right of the turret of the T70, at the bottom center is the fuel filler cap cover for the auxiliary generator. The weld seams of the turret are noticeable. The turret armor was 1.5 inches thick at the front and ½ inch thick at the sides.

The top of the hull to the front of the turret is viewed from the right side. Beyond the filler cap are the co-driver's hatch doors. The cage-shaped structure beyond these doors at the top center of the glacis was a guard for a siren that is missing.

The barrel of the 76mm gun fits snugly through the gun shield. To the side of telescope shield is the vertically oriented casting number for the gun shield. Behind the gun shield is the mounting plate, with lifting rings for removing the gun mount.

This bulge, present on the left side of the turret up through M18 serial number 34, was intended to provide clearance for the operating mechanism of the 76mm gun. When the gun was later rotated, the bulge on the turret wall was discontinued.

A curved section of armor forming part of the foundation of the ring mount for the .50-caliber machine gun is welded to the wall of the left side of the turret. The weld seams taper toward the top, with as many as six weld seams being visible at the bottom.

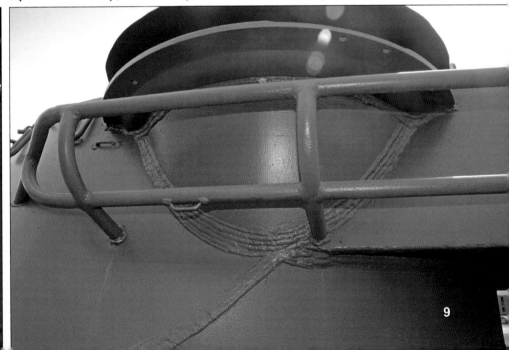

9

The breech of the earliest T70 vehicles' M1 cannon was mounted in a vertical position as shown here. Bulges in the turret sides provided clearance for the crew to operate the weapon. (Patton Museum via Steve Zaloga)

Later vehicles mounted the cannon at a slight angle, thus eliminating the need for the bulges in the turret sides. This arrangement simplified production and provided better protection for the crew. (Patton Museum via Steve Zaloga)

Following tests of the M70 in June 1943, the vehicle was accepted and quickly went into production under the designation 76mm Gun Motor Carriage (GMC) M18. Buick completed the first production examples of the M18 in July 1943. Almost immediately, minor problems were discovered with components such as the transmission and suspension, which were fixed through a series of modifications. This fully running example of an M18 in the collection of Brent Mullins utilizes T85E1 tracks normally found on the M24 Chaffee.

In addition to the driver, this vehicle is crewed by a man standing at the commander's position at the ring-mounted Browning M2 .50-caliber machine gun, and another man standing at the loader's position to the right of the 76mm gun. On the left fender are markings for Company C, 807th Tank Destroyer Battalion, of the Seventh Armored Division. The orange-yellow insignia on the side of the hull is that of the Tank Destroyer Force.

This M18 nicknamed *Cocky* is in the collection of Fred Ropkey. Unit markings on the fenders are for Company C, 603rd Tank Destroyer Battalion, 6th Armored Division. The vehicle lacks the sand shields, which operational experience proved to be fragile.

The left headlight assembly and brush guard of the M18 at the Military History Institute, serial number 661, are viewed from the front. The base of the headlight is welded to the glacis. To the left is one of the lifting eyes on top of the engine-access door.

The left headlight assembly and its brush guard are viewed from an angle. The headlight assembly consists of a service headlight with a blackout marker light on top. In the background are the siren, its brush guard, and the right headlight and guard.

On the oblique armor plate at the upper left front of the hull is an oblong access plate, secured in place with 12 hex screws. Removal of the plate provided access to the connections at the rear of the instrument panel in the driver's compartment.

Emblazoned on the left side of this 76mm GMC M18 is the insignia of the Tank Destroyer Force. It consists of a likeness of a black panther crushing a tank in its jaws, inside a yellow-orange circular background.

The top left corner of the hull is viewed, with the left fender to the lower left and the driver's hatch doors to the right. In the foreground is one of the several tow cable holders that were positioned around the top of the hull, to hold the tow cable neatly in place.

The top of the left fender of the 76mm GMC M18 in the collection of Fred Ropkey is displayed, showing how the top of the fender is welded to the hull, and the front-and-side skirt of the fender is attached to the top of the fender with hex screws.

While the pilot T70s had driver's (seen here) and co-driver's doors with laterally split forward and rear panels, production M18s like this one had two-panel doors with a front-to-rear joint between them. The outboard doors had a periscope on a rotary mount.

A Browning Automatic Rifle is visible below the 76mm gun barrel in this view of part of the front left section of the Ropkey M18. On the side of the turret is a bin for storing the driver's detachable hood, which could be installed over his hatch during foul weather, enabling him to poke his head through the hatch and not have to navigate by using his periscope. The thin, vertical metal strip on the turret to the front of the bin for the driver's hood was one of several strips for attaching a dust cover over the gun and gun shield.

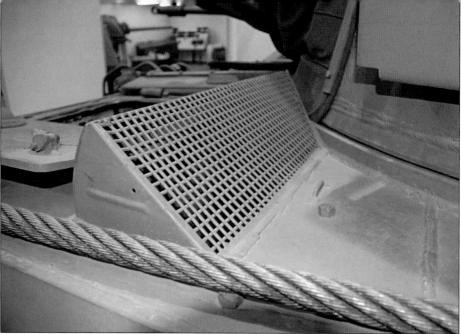

The pie-shaped side of the cowl of the air-outlet vent had a horizontal stiffener stamped in it. A belt-driven fan pulled air from inside the fighting compartment past the transmission and differential oil coolers, under the floor, and out this vent.

A driver's hood is stored in the bin on the side of the turret. This view also illustrates the arrangement of the M18's running gear, including five sets of road wheels per side and four track-support rollers (also called track-return roller) above the road wheels.

Like the M18 in the preceding photograph, the M18 in the collection of Brent Mullins has the raised air-outlet vent for the transmission and differential oil coolers, immediately aft of the driver's hatch, comprising a cowl and grille.

Like the drive sprockets of the T70 pilot vehicles, the drive sprockets of the M18 had 31 teeth, with every other recess between teeth. The sprocket and the final-drive assembly were equipped with a compensating linkage to maintain the proper track tension.

Tracks engaged with the left sprocket of an M18 are viewed. These are the T69 single-pin tracks, a center-guide, rubber-bushed design with a width of 12 inches (14⅜ inches inclusive of the track pins) and a pitch (front-to-rear measurement) of 5.09 inches.

A tow cable keeper on top of the hull adjacent to the left side of the turret is in the foreground. Below it and to the rear, on the side of the hull, are footman loops for securing detachable bore-cleaning staffs for the 76mm main gun. All U.S. armored vehicles were supplied with tow cables for rapid recovery of mired or disabled vehicles.

The rear set of footman loops on the left side of an M18 are viewed close-up. Straps would be secured to these loops and tightened over the bore-cleaning staffs to stow them. The vertical strip of steel served as a stopper, to keep the staffs from shifting around.

A view of the same M18 shown in the preceding photo was taken on the left side slightly to the rear of the area shown in the preceding view. Welded to the side of the hull above and forward of the footman loop is a bracket for stowing a crow bar.

The ends of three bore-cleaning staffs are viewed close-up. The top two have metal threaded male ends, while the bottom staff has a metal socket. Next to these ends is the retainer bracket that kept the staffs from shifting around in their retainer straps.

A complement of bore-cleaning staffs is stowed on the side of an M18. They have threaded fittings for assembling them into a single, long staff. An M15 bore-cleaning brush would be fitted to the end of the staff for scrubbing the inside of the barrel.

A steel crowbar is in its stowed position toward the rear of the left side of the hull of an M18. It rests on two holders and is secured by two straps. To the front and rear of the crowbar are retainer brackets for keeping the crowbar from shifting around.

The standing figure in the machine gun ring mount of Brent Mullins's 76mm GMC M18 gives a sense of the fairly small scale and low profile of this type of vehicle. Visible markings include the U.S. Army registration number 40145397 toward the rear of the hull, markings the 807th Tank Destroyer Battalion of the 7th Army, on the left of the rear of the hull, and markings for the 24th vehicle in Company C on the right of the rear of the hull. Stowed on the rear of the hull are a shovel, a pick-axe head, and a hand crank for manually rotating the engine and clearing oil from the lower cylinders before starting.

At the lower rear of the hull of the M18 are two angle irons. These are welded to the engine-access door and serve as a reinforced mounting for the towing pintle at the center of the angle irons. Tow hooks are mounted to the sides of the rear of the hull.

The towing pintle on the Military History Institute's 76mm GMC M18 is viewed from the right side. The facets of the I-beams that hold the tow hook grow wider at the center, as seen here. Each end of each I-beam is fastened to the hull with two hex screws.

The towing pintle is attached rigidly to a mounting plate welded to the angle irons that run across the lower part of the rear of the hull. Four hex screws secure the towing pintle to the plate. This vehicle is the Military History Institute's 76mm GMC M18.

The right rear tow hook of the M18 at the Military History Institute is observed close-up. It is secured in place with a pin and cotter pins. To the upper right is the hex track-adjusting nut for moving the idler wheel forward and rearward to adjust track tension.

Spare track links were stored on the rear of the turret: a measure that also provided a bit of extra protection. The track pins fit through holes in the top and bottom retainers, and the tracks could be removed by removing the top retainer.

The left side of the rear deck of the hull of the Ropkey 76mm GMC M18 is in view. A pickaxe handle is stored on two brackets, with a retainer adjacent to the end of the handle. Also on the deck is the left fuel filler cap cover. To the right is the stowed crowbar.

The spare-track storage arrangement on the rear of the turret featured on both the T70 pilot vehicles and the production M18s. The two hinges visible at the turret's top edge are for the access door on top of the turret for the stowage box in the rear of the bustle.

On each side of the rear deck is a latch for securing the ends of the tow cable. This latch is shown closed, but not locked. A toggle bolt and wing nut are provided to lock the latch over the cable. Just aft of the latch is the oil tank filler screen door with two hinges.

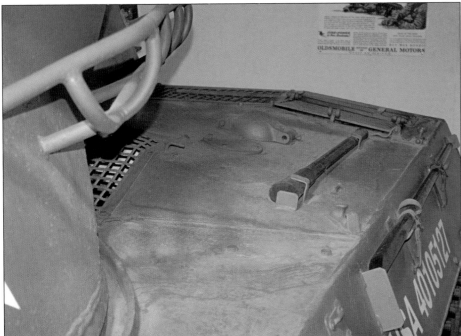

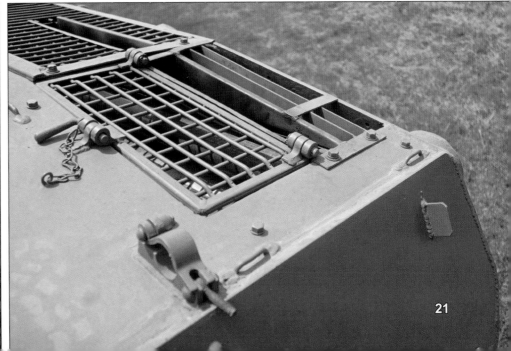

The oil tank filler screen door near the left rear corner of the rear deck of the Military History Institute's M18 is observed, with the front of the door to the top. The grilles are formed of criss-crossing rods, the fore-and-aft rods positioned under the lateral rods.

The engine rests in a support anchored to the hull in alignment with the transfer case at the front of the engine compartment. Four rollers on the bottom of the support rest on tracks, allowing the engine to be removed easily by rolling it out of the rear hull door.

The engine compartment door on the rear deck of the Military History Institute's M18 is open, revealing the engine exhaust lines. Between the exhausts, the cup-shaped fixture with the top secured with a wing nut is the engine crankcase breather assembly.

Engine Data

ENGINE MAKE/MODEL*	Continental R975-C1	Continental R975-C4
NUMBER OF CYLINDERS	9 radial	9 radial
CUBIC INCH DISPLACEMENT	973	973
HORSEPOWER	350 @ 2,400	400 @ 2,400
TORQUE	840 @ 1,700	940 @ 1,700
GOVERNED SPEED	2,400 rpm	2,400 rpm

• Serial numbers 1 through 1350 used the naturally-aspirated Continental R975-C1, later vehicles used the supercharged R975-C4

M18 Registration and Serial Numbers

Production Order	Quantity	Reg. Number	Serial Number
RAD-563	6	40128384-40128389	Pilot models
T-6641	1,000	40108110-40109109	1-1000
T-9167	1,507	40144883-40146389	1007-2513

Elements of the rear of the engine of the Military History Institute's 76mm GMC M18 are viewed from above. Prominent toward the lower right is the starter, featuring a 24-volt, 4-pole compound, intermittent-duty motor mounted on the engine crankcase, and equipped with an auxiliary mechanism for hand-cranking the engine starter. The white object at the top left is a fire extinguisher horn (or nozzle) and its support; there were six such horns in the engine compartment: two at the front and four at the rear.

The rear of the rear deck of the M18 in the Fred Ropkey collection is displayed. Running across the deck are the right air outlet grille (foreground) and the center air outlet grille, the wider grille in the background. These grilles are constructed of a mix of vertical slats or criss-crossing rods enclosed in frames. Below the grilles at the aft end of the engine compartment is the muffler and exhaust assembly. Situated above the mufflers are the tail pipes, with slotted exhaust ports.

The rear and right side of the turret of the M18 is viewed from over the right rear of the hull. Protruding from the top of the turret is the mount for a radio antenna. To the right are a machine gun tripod and the tripod stowage bracket.

A tripod for a Browning M2 .50-caliber machine gun is shown in its stored position on the right rear of the hull deck of an M18. Adjacent to the tripod is the armored cover for the right-hand fuel tank filler. This tank held 90 gallons, versus 75 gallons for the left.

From the right rear the placement of the .50-caliber machine gun tripod in its stowage bracket on the rear deck is visible. Also in view is part of the right idler wheel, or compensating wheel, and the shock absorber for the rear road wheel.

A sledgehammer is stored on the right side of the 76mm GMC M18; it rests on two brackets and is secured in place with a leather strap and buckle. Above the sledgehammer are the two rear legs of the tripod and their retainer latch.

An axe is stored on the right side of the hull of the M18, adjacent to the turret. The head of the axe and the handle rest on different brackets, and an adjustable leather retainer strap with a buckle, wrapped through a footman loop, secures the axe in place.

On the 76MM GMC M18, the fuel-filler cap cover for the auxiliary generator's fuel tank and the ventilator hood and exhaust pipe (lower left) for the auxiliary generator are viewed facing to the rear. In the background is the right front of the turret.

Brent Mullins's 76mm GMC M18 performs at his military vehicle show, with another 76mm GMC M18 in the background. A canvas dust cover is present over the gun shield. The respective positions of the headlights and siren are apparent.

The right headlight and brush guard of an M18 are viewed from above. On the right side of the brush guard is a holder for storing a plug with a retainer chain for inserting into the headlight mounting sleeve when the headlight is removed.

The right headlight assembly on a 76mm GMC M18 is viewed from the front. The holder for the headlight mounting-sleeve plug is present on the brush guard but not the retainer chain. To the upper right are the vehicle's siren and its brush guard.

The arrangement of the right service headlight with the small blackout marker light mounted on top is displayed on the Military History Institute's M18, serial number 661. Behind the service headlight, the holder and retainer chain for the plug is visible.

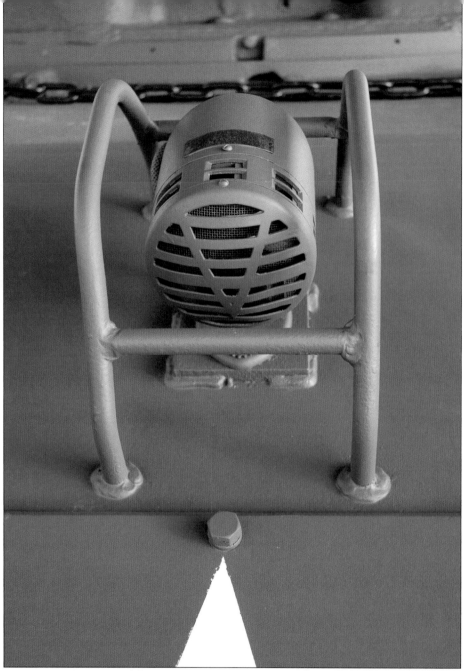

Mounted on the top center of the glacis, above the transmission access door, is an electric siren. On top of the body of the siren is a small nomenclature plate. The siren's brush guard is made of two steel rods bent into bow shapes, with the legs neatly welded to the glacis and with two horizontal rods welded to the bows. The base plate of the siren is welded to the glacis.

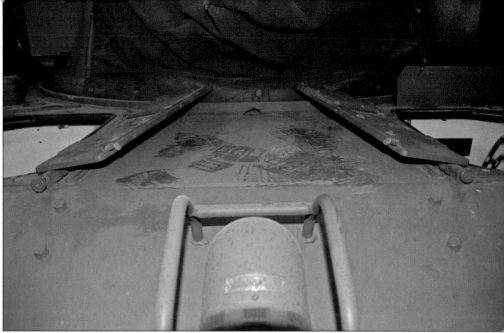

The siren is shown in its location at the top center of the glacis on the 76mm GMC M18. The siren is pointed downward, more or less parallel with the slope of the glacis. Visible to the right on the glacis is a tow cable keeper.

With the top of the siren in the foreground, the top deck of the hull to the front of the turret is displayed, footprints visible in the dust on it. The inboard panels of the driver's (right) and co-driver's doors are open.

The left side of the dust cover over the gun shield is displayed. It was constructed of heavy-duty, sewn canvas. It is secured to the turret with metal strips such as the one to the right. The gunner's telescope shield appears through a cutout.

The gunner's telescope shield on the gun shield of the 76mm GMC M18 is viewed close-up. The gunner opened the telescope shield by means of an operating rod pulling on the small arm extending from the upper inboard corner of the cover.

As seen from the left side, the shield, or mantlet, of the main gun is of relatively thin profile. The bulged armor section on the turret to the rear of the gun shield is the mounting plate, with a lifting eye to each side. The telescope shield is visible in profile.

The right sides of the gun shield and rotor shield of the 76mm GMC M18 at the Military History Institute are viewed. The raised object on the upper right of the gun shield is a casting number, 350. In the foreground are a hatch hood stowage bin and a lifting eye.

The rotor shield (left) and the gun shield (right) on the 76mm GMC M18 are observed from the right side of the vehicle, looking downward. Casting marks are faintly visible on top of the gun shield. In the background, the operating rod of the gunner's telescope shield can be seen exiting through a hole in the gun shield. The front end of the operating rod is connected to the arm extending from the top of the inboard side of the telescope shield.

The open-topped turret of the M18 is observed from overhead facing to the rear. The ring mount for the .50-caliber machine gun is to the upper right. To the left of the photo is a cover over the right turret box.

Running across the top front of the turret is a cowl containing the gunner's M4A1 periscope and a grab bar. The driver's hatch hood is stored in the bin on the left side of the turret. The top retainer strip of the dust cover of the gun shield is at the lower left.

More of the cowl across the front of the turret is visible on the M18. The two pairs of thin metal strips protruding from the cowl are sighting vanes, used for roughly aligning the gun on a target. To the left, part of the main gun's travel lock is visible.

The main gun's travel lock at the upper center of the photo is viewed from the right side of the turret. Mounted to the cover over the right turret box, the lock swung down and was latched to a lug on the recoil cylinder to hold the gun stationary when traveling.

In an overhead view of the M18's turret, the travel lock is at the upper center, and the 76mm gun is to the left. To the bottom right is a grab bar for the use of the loader when standing up. Around the rim at the bottom left are several crash pads.

The travel lock of the 76mm gun on the M18 is viewed from the rear. This was the early type of travel lock, later supplanted by a more sophisticated one. When not engaged with the 76mm gun, it was pinned to a lug on top of the right ammunition box.

The design of the bin for the co-driver's hatch hood on the right side of the turret of the M18 is shown. The sides are welded to the turret, as is the shelf that partially encloses the bottom but leaves spaces for water to escape.

The co-driver's hood is stored in its bin on the M18. The weatherproof canvas part of the hood is against the turret. On the metal frame of the hood is a windshield wiper. Similar hoods were available for the driver and the co-driver.

The top of the co-driver's hood is viewed in its stowage bin. On the upper part of the side of the turret are several of the U-shaped brackets for supporting the soft top that could be placed over the turret during foul weather.

The rear and right rear of the turret of the 76mm GMC M18, including the spare-track stowage, are displayed. Also in view is the manner of attaching the rear of the stowage rack to the side of the turret. To the lower left is the engine compartment door.

Whereas the T70 pilot vehicles had a curved section of armor extending from the left side of the turret to form a foundation for the outboard part of the machine gun ring mount, production M18s had that bulge formed integrally with the left side of the turret.

The bulge under the machine gun ring mount is viewed on the M18 at the Military History Institute. A casting number, upside down, is visible on the ring. Footman loops are welded to the bottom rail of the stowage rack, for attaching hold-down straps.

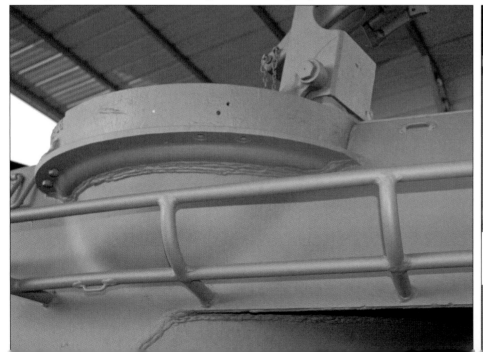

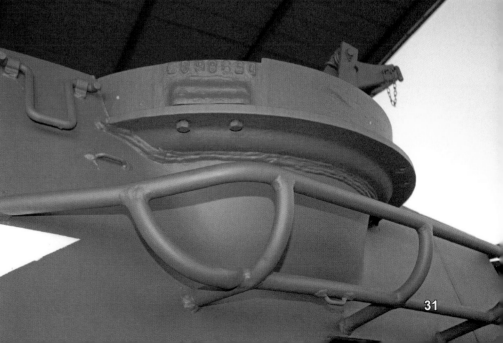

The .50-caliber machine gun ring mount on the M18 turret is viewed from overhead, with the rear of the turret to the left. To the right is the gun support, positioned on an inner ring that rotated on ball bearings on the outer, stationary ring.

This is one of two small supports that the commander of the vehicle would push his upper body against to rotate the ring mount. This one has a cushion attached to the metal frame, whereas the two cradles visible in the preceding photo lack those cushions.

A Browning M2 .50-caliber machine gun is emplaced on the ring mount of this M18, as well as a .50-caliber ammunition box with a capacity of 105 rounds. The ammunition box rests on a tray attached to the machine gun's carriage.

Looking down into the ring mount of the M18, the right cradle of the mount is toward the top. The rear of the turret is toward the right. Inside the turret below the ring mount is the round seat for the commander and, to its front, the gunner's seat.

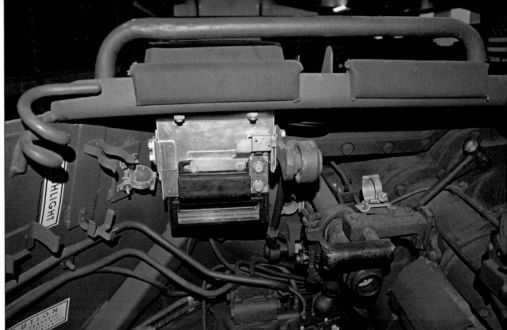

On the left wall of a late-production M18 turret are some of the gunner's controls. Below the flashlight sign in the middle is the azimuth indicator, to the right of which is the traverse gear box, atop which is the traverse motor, with hydraulic lines feeding into it.

This is a gunner's forward view in the turret of an M18. To the left of center is the gunner's periscope, with crash pads on the rim of the cowl above the periscope. Below and to the right of the periscope is the T76 telescope, for direct fire.

One of the idiosyncrasies of the M18 is that the 76mm main gun and its M1 gun mount were installed with the breech tilted at 45 degrees, to make it easier to load the gun in the cramped confines of the turret. The 76mm gun shown here is the M1A1C.

The breech of the 76mm gun M1A1C in an M18 is viewed close-up. The breechblock is the sliding type. The loader stood to the right of the gun, retrieved ready rounds of ammunition from the rack to the right, and inserted them in the breech.

Mounted at an angle in the sponson to the left of the driver's position is his instrument panel. At the top center are switches for the booster, magneto, and starter. Below those switches are two large gauges: the engine tachometer and engine oil temperature.

To the left of the co-driver's seat (visible at the bottom of the photo) is the housing for the Torqmatic transmission, with three forward gears and one reverse gear. To the right, with the "flashlight" placard, is the guard over the right final-drive universal joint.

The co-driver's seat is visible through his hatch, with the front of the vehicle to the top. A rubber weather seal is mounted around the perimeter of the hatch. On the right panel of the hatch doors are two locking handles and the periscope on a rotary mount.

In a view from the co-driver's perspective, the silver-colored bar at the top of the compartment is the cross-shaft co-driver's steering levers. Below the right end of the cross-shaft is a spare periscope heads box. To the right is a fire extinguisher.

FLASHLIGHT

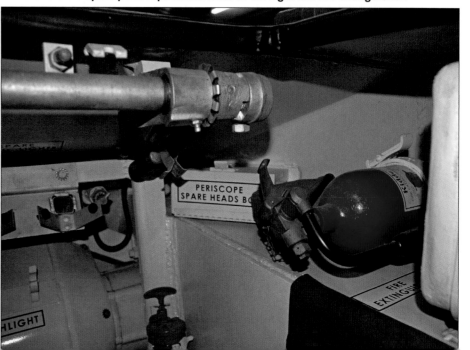

PERISCOPE SPARE HEADS BOX

FIRE EXTINGUISHER

HLIGHT

HLIGHT

A roadworthy 76mm GMC M18 photographed in Europe carries a full load of extra equipment, from camouflage netting draped over the front of the hull to extra ammunition boxes and spare tracks on the glacis and rucksacks on the turret. (Pierre-Olivier Buan)

This M18 is equipped with the 76mm gun M1A1C, distinguished by the thread-protecting ring fitted on the muzzle. The dust cover is not installed over the gun, permitting a clear view of the design of the gun mantlet on this vehicle. (Pierre-Olivier Buan)

The rear of the hull of this M18 tank destroyer has been tricked out with a rack for stowing 5-gallon liquid containers. This vehicle has also been refitted with T85E1 rubber-chevron tracks and corresponding drive sprockets. (Pierre-Olivier Buan)

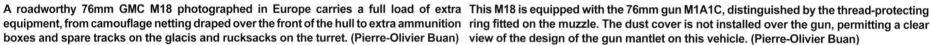

Barrel Development

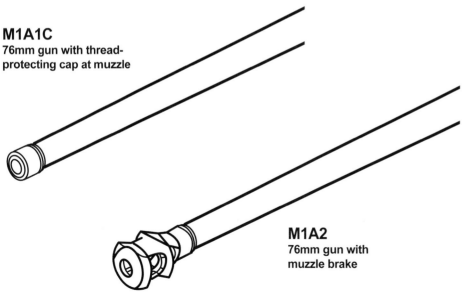

M1A1C
76mm gun with thread-protecting cap at muzzle

M1A2
76mm gun with muzzle brake

This late-production 76mm GMC M18, nicknamed *Rachel,* belongs to Steve Preston. It features a 76mm gun M1A2, identifiable by its muzzle brake. Another noticeable feature is the flush-mounted air-outlet vent for the transmission and differential oil coolers, located just behind the driver's hatch. This vent replaced the raised air-outlet vent in the same location found on the pilot M70 vehicles and early M18s. This vehicle lacks the front and rear sand shields, which were often removed from M18s and discarded during World War II. (James Alexander)

The M18 has the 31-tooth drive sprockets with large lightening holes that had been employed on these vehicles since the T70 pilots. Red grease fittings are present on the hubs of the road wheels and the track-support wheels. (James Alexander)

The dual shock absorbers for the front road wheel are visible above that wheel on a very late M18. Faulty shock absorbers were a significant problem with the T70s and early M18s, but during production, improved shock absorbers were substituted.

The forward left dual track-support roller, or track-return roller, of this M18 is in view. The track-support rollers, as well as the road wheels, were fitted with solid vulcanized-rubber tires. A good view is offered of the track center guides.

The M18 road wheels mounted 26 x 4.5 inch vulcanized rubber tires. The road wheels were individually sprung on torsion bars, and all road wheels but the center ones had shock absorbers.

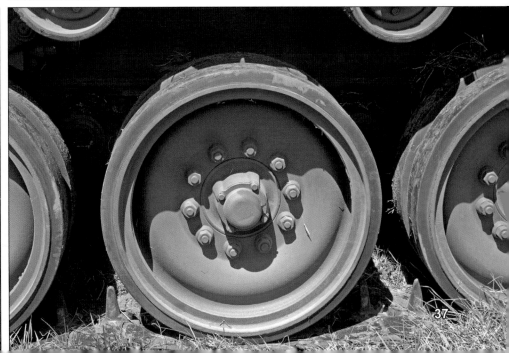

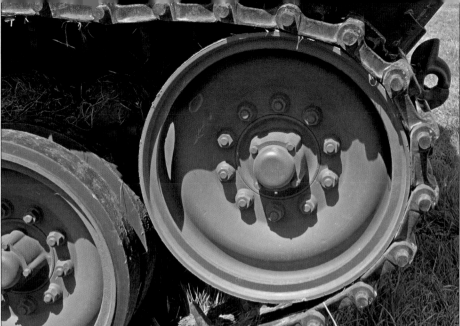

Road wheels on the left side of an M18 are shown. Two of the suspension arms are visible where they join the hull, and they are connected to torsion bars mounted across the bottom of the hull. (James Alexander)

Mounted at the rear of the hull on each side is a dual idler wheel. The idler wheels were 23.5 x 4.5 inches and were adjustable in order to properly tension the tracks. They were not fitted with rubber tires.

A late M18 restored by Marc Sehring for Allan Cors, in the collection of the National Museum of Americans in Wartime, demonstrates the torsion bar suspension and high speed capability for which the Hellcat is noteworthy. The Hellcat's radial engine, of aircraft origin. could push the vehicle to speeds over 55 miles per hour. (Scott Taylor)

The 805th Tank Destroyer Battalion employed distinctive markings on its M18 76mm Gun Motor Carriages in northern Italy from at least September 1944 to April 1945. These markings included the black panther Tank Destroyer insignia and tactical signs indicating the platoon and vehicle number.

Rachel, the late-production 76mm GMC M18 in the collection of Steve Preston, was completed quite late in the M18 production run. It is fitted with T69 tracks and the original 31-tooth drive sprockets. Markings on the fenders are for the third vehicle of Company B, 805th Tank Destroyer Battalion, Fifth Army. The gunner's telescope shield is shown open. The front of the canvas dust cover, through which the gunner's telescope shield protrudes, is secured around the 76mm gun barrel with a strap. (James Alexander)

Stowed along with the bore-cleaning staffs on the left side of the hull are three red-and-white-striped aiming stakes, used for establishing the azimuth of the gun when the vehicle was conducting an indirect-fire mission.

In this overhead view of the middle part of the upper hull of an M18, the tow cable is secured by one of the several cable keepers, open-topped brackets welded to the hull. Details of the turret ring are also in view. On the edge of the hull are aiming stakes and bore-cleaning staffs. (James Alexander)

To use the aiming stakes, one stake was pushed into the ground at least 50 yards from the vehicle, and another stake was set at least 50 yards beyond the near stake. The gunner placed his sights on the stakes and set his azimuth indicator at zero. (James Alexander)

The ends of the bore-cleaning staffs are viewed close-up. These are the treaded, male ends, which would screw into socket ends on the assembled staff. The points at the bottoms of the two aiming stakes, also called aiming posts, are also illustrated.

The driver's hatch doors of a late M18 are shown open. The driver's periscope is on the outboard panel of the doors. The small, round fixtures next to the front hinges of the doors are door latch knobs, which engage lugs on the doors to lock them open.

As seen here from overhead, the outboard door of the driver's hatch is fitted with a crash pad, two locking handles, and an M6 periscope in a rotary mount. The aluminum-colored knob on the periscope mount was for adjusting and locking the periscope.

The driver's hood is shown installed on the M18. It provided just enough room for him to raise his head above the hatch. The windshield wiper was powered by a wire plugged into a 24-volt receptacle inside the crew compartment. (James Alexander)

The driver's and co-driver's hoods are held in place by two rods with wing nuts at the top. The wires running across the inside of the windshield are electrical defrosting wires. The windshield wiper blade is missing on this hood. (James Alexander)

The canvas part of the driver's hood was held down on the perimeter of the hatch by gravity, with no snaps or other means to secure it in place. Details of the periscope and periscope mount are visible, as well as the door latch knob. (James Alexander)

Several equipment bags are stowed on the rack on the left side of this turret bustle. The latch for securing the tow cable and, to the lower right, the oil tank filler screen door and the left air outlet grille are also in view.

The late-type, flush-mounted air-outlet vent for the transmission and differential oil coolers comprised 10 fins oriented fore-and-aft, underneath which is a an expanded-steel grille. The grille is not flat but is formed in a cupped or scooped shape.

Stored on the rear left portion of the hull are a crowbar and a pickaxe handle. Next to handle is the armored cover for the filler cap of the left fuel tank, and next to the cover is the flush-fitting fuel-tank gauge cover.

A very late-production M18 advances across a field. Reenactors wearing period-correct crash helmets man the turret. Although an engine-starter crank is present on the rear of the hull, and a tow cable is stored on top of the hull, other typical pieces of accessory equipment, such as bore-cleaning staff, crowbar, shovel, pickaxe handle, and .50-caliber machine gun tripod are not mounted. Six spare track links are stored in the racks at the rear of the turret bustle.

This overhead view of the rear deck of a 76mm GMC M18 shows the mufflers and exhaust underneath the air outlet grilles at the rear of the deck. Gaps in the grilles allowed a clear space for exhaust gasses to escape. Air circulating out of these grilles helped blow the exhaust fumes clear of the vehicle. Immediately forward of the center air outlet grille is the engine access door, referred to in M18 technical manuals as the hull rear roof door. (James Alexander)

A late-production 76mm GMC M18 displays an external complement of standard on-vehicle equipment, including a shovel, machine gun tripod with a canvas cover (to protect the cradle and leg hinges), sledgehammer, and axe. Also, stowed on the racks on the sides of the turret bustle are a rolled-up camouflage net (right) and M1935 officer bed rolls (left). From this angle, the bustle of the turret completely hides the air inlet grilles, located on the rear deck to the front of the engine access door. (James Alexander)

Visible in this photo is the angled demarcation between the upper part of the rear of the hull and the lower part of the rear of the hull. A shovel is shown stowed in its brackets and secured with a russet leather strap. (James Alexander)

In a view of the rear of Bill Bauer's very late-production M18, to the left is the bracket for holding the shovel blade, and to the right is the D-shaped holder for the shovel handle. The two footman loops are for the shovel-retainer strap.

On the engine-access door on the rear of the hull are stowed the hand starter crank for the engine and a pickaxe head. The design of the tow pintle and its mounting is similar to that of earlier-production M18s depicted earlier in this book. (James Alexander)

The rear of the hull of an M18 is displayed, with emphasis on the angle-iron stiffeners running across the engine-access door. These angle irons are welded at intervals to the door. Two hex bolts at the end of each angle iron secures it to the hull.

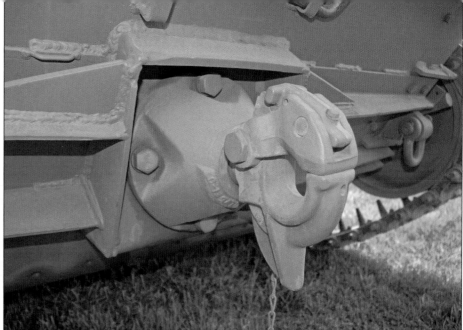

Unlike the fixed tow pintle found on most M18 Gun Motor Carriages, the very late production vehicles feature a pintle hook mounted on a round, swiveling mount, that allows the hook to flex when towing a trailer over rough ground.

A box-like weldment encloses the mount for the tow pintle on this M18. The hex screws that secure the tow pintle mount in place were originally secured in place by locking wires, which were wrapped around the shanks of the screws below the hex heads.

The rear hull door of this M18 is lowered, exposing the engine compartment. Above and below the tow hook lugs, a bracket is welded to the hull, tapped with two holes for securing the angle irons on the door with screws.

The first 1,350 M18s had the Continental R975-C1 radial engine, and late M18s such as this one had the R975-C4. At the bottom center is the carburetor, with air inlet tubes to each side of it. The carburetor was not interchangeable on the -C1 and -C4 engines.

In addition to the box-shaped weldment that surrounds the mount for the towing pintle, triangular gussets have been welded to the upper sides of the box and the angle irons. Stowed on the rear plate is the engine crank, used to clear the lower cylinders of oil.

The M18's power-operated turret allows the 76mm main gun to be brought to bear through 360 degrees. Here the muzzle brake is nearly over the rear plate of the hull, where the engine crank handle, shovel and mattock head are stowed. (James Alexander)

The rubber tires on the three rear road wheel assemblies on the right side of a late M18 exhibit fairly smooth sidewalls and pitted, dirt-stained outer rims, including a few significant gouges. Also in view are two track-support wheel assemblies.

Secured to the right side of the rear deck of this late M18 is a machine gun tripod with canvas mount cover. Also in the view are the right fuel filler cap cover and fuel gauge cover, and, under the grille, the right side of the exhaust. (James Alexander)

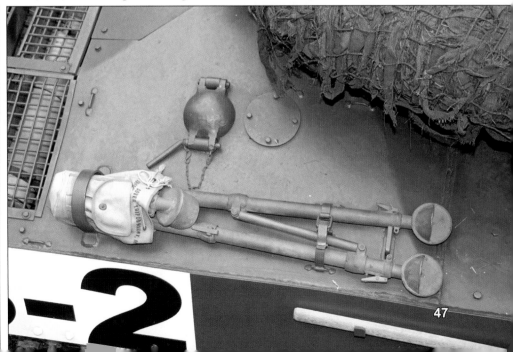

The Tank Destroyer Force insignia stands out prominently on the front of the hull in this overhead view of the right side of Steve Preston's M18, nicknamed *Rachel*. From above, the relative thinness of the armor on the turret is apparent. The turret armor was a mix of rolled and cast homogenous steel. The sides and rear of the turret were ½ inch thick and were set at an angle of 20 degrees. The front of the turret and the turret shield were 1.5 inches thick. The hull armor varied in thickness from a maximum of 1.75 inches on the lower front to a minimum of 0.5 inches on the top deck and the floor. (James Alexander)

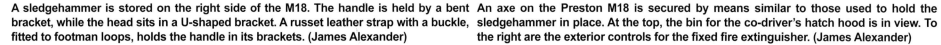

A sledgehammer is an indispensable tool when maintaining an armored fighting vehicle, especially when replacing damaged track shoes.

An axe is part of the basic pioneer tool kit furnished with virtually all US military vehicles.

A sledgehammer is stored on the right side of the M18. The handle is held by a bent bracket, while the head sits in a U-shaped bracket. A russet leather strap with a buckle, fitted to footman loops, holds the handle in its brackets. (James Alexander)

An axe on the Preston M18 is secured by means similar to those used to hold the sledgehammer in place. At the top, the bin for the co-driver's hatch hood is in view. To the right are the exterior controls for the fixed fire extinguisher. (James Alexander)

The 76mm GMC M18 had the advantages of speed, maneuverability, a low profile, and an excellent antitank gun. On the debit side, its light armor left it vulnerable, and, as can be seen here, its open-topped turret left the crew exposed to sniper fire, hand grenades, and artillery air bursts. An armored roof developed for the turret found its way onto a number of M18s. Another shortcoming was the vehicle's lack of a coaxial machine gun, which would have allowed the M18 to engage targets not worth firing 76mm ammunition at.

The name *Darthy* was inscribed forward of the U.S. Army registration number, 40108864, on this M18 serving with the 827th Tank Destroyer Battalion, an African-American unit in the 12th Armored Division, at Sarrebourg, France, at the end of 1944. Marked under the axe is "B-10," and toward the front of the sponson is "9604-V."

Bill Bauer's very late production 76mm GMC M18 drives down a ramp at the end of a Bailey bridge, a type of prefabricated portable truss bridge developed by the British early in World War II. A good view is available of the double-baffle muzzle brake of the 76mm gun M1A2, which was installed on fewer than 700 M18s during the final months of production in the summer of 1944. The muzzle brake both countered the recoil forces of the gun and reduced the amount of dust kicked up when firing, enabling the gunner to set up his next shot better.

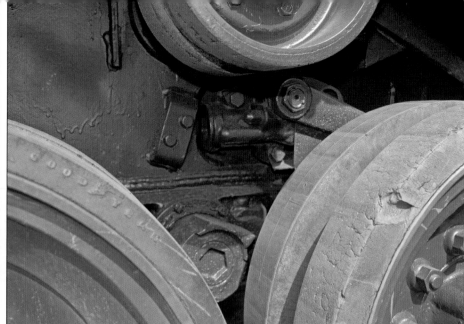

The T69 tracks engage the recess between every other tooth on the sprocket. The part of the track that engages the sprocket is the track pin, which extends 1 3/16 inches from each side of the 12-inch-wide body of the track.

In a view between the front road wheel and the second-from-front road wheel on the right side, below the track-support roller is part of one of the shock absorbers for the front road wheel; the other shock for that wheel is at the upper right.

Visible between the right idler wheel (left) and the rear road wheel is the shock absorber for the rear road wheel. During production of the M18, shock-absorber failure was a continuing problem until stronger shocks were developed.

The exhaust pipe for the auxiliary generator is tack-welded to the side of the hull and is set at a rearward angle, its outlet at the bottom. The four hex screws near the bottom of the upper plate of the hull were for fastening the two-piece forward track guard.

The position and design of the external actuator handles and housing for the fixed fire extinguisher system and the vent hood and exhaust for the auxiliary generator remained virtually unchanged from those on the T70 pilot vehicles seen earlier in this book.

Embossed on the handles is the instruction, "fire – pull hard." Safety wires helped prevent accidental discharge, and seals on the safety wires indicate the discharge status of the extinguishers.

The name *Hot Stuff!* was painted in white on the front of the sponson of an M18 Hellcat assigned to the 602nd Tank Destroyer Battalion. Among its other combat activities, this vehicle and its unit supported the 89th Infantry Division in fighting around Sankt Goar, Germany, in March 1945. A stowage container is on the rear of the turret bustle.

The driver's head is visible poking through the hatch of this M18. The front-hull door, all of which is visible here, is assembled from three pieces of steel welded together at two horizontal joints. The door is secured to the front of the hull with hex screws. The end of the tow cable is tied with a bit of rope to one of two lifting eyes on the top of the front-hull door.

In this overhead view of an M18 the design of the top of the muzzle brake is visible. The ports through which the gasses from firing the gun escaped point to the sides. This feature deflected the gasses from venting downward at the ground, thus reducing the amount of dust stirred up when firing the main gun. A Browning M2 .50-caliber machine gun is present on the ring mount. This weapon's main stated purpose on the M18 was for antiaircraft defense, but it was often used against ground targets. (James Alexander)

Although the driver's and co-driver's hatch hoods are stored in their bins on the turret, in actual service these hoods were often omitted, and other equipment was stowed in the bins. (James Alexander)

The shape of the front of the muzzle brake on the M18 is shown. The M1A2 gun depicted had rifling of 32 grooves with a uniform right-hand twist, with one full turn per 32 calibers. The earlier M1A1 gun had one turn per 40 calibers. (James Alexander)

The right headlight assembly has the large, sealed-beam service headlight mounted upon a support bracket. The direction of the service headlight could be adjusted to properly aim its illumination. Positioned above the service headlight is the blackout marker light. On the rear of the right leg of the brush guard is the holder for the headlight-socket plug. Attached to the plug is a retainer chain. These lights could be quickly removed and stowed in the driver's compartment to prevent damage. (James Alexander)

The siren on the M18 produced sound by rotating T-shaped blades within a stationary stator at high speeds. The driver turned the siren on and off by pressing a push-type button with his left foot. The M18 technical manual recommended testing the siren for tone and proper operation on a regular basis, when the tactical situation permitted. The mounting bracket for the siren is tack welded to the glacis at the corners of the bracket. A brush guard protects the siren from damage. (James Alexander)

The left headlight assembly is similar in design and layout to the right headlight. This shows the normal service headlight. When the vehicle had to drive under blackout conditions, a blackout service headlight configuration was available for the left headlight, in which case the normal headlight assembly was removed and the blackout headlight assembly was installed. Headlight assemblies were removed by releasing a lock in the driver's compartment and pulling them free. When not in use, the blackout light was stowed in the driver's compartment. (James Alexander)

Specifications

MODEL	M18
WEIGHT	37,557 pounds
LENGTH*	262 inches
WIDTH*	113 inches
HEIGHT*	101 inches
CREW	5
MAXIMUM SPEED	45 mph
FUEL CAPACITY	170 gallons
RANGE	105 miles
ELECTRICAL	24 negative
TRANSMISSION SPEEDS	3 forward / 1 rear
TRANSFER SPEEDS	1
TURNING RADIUS	33 feet
ARMAMENT, MAIN	76mm
ARMAMENT, SECONDARY	1 x .50 cal. M2 Browning
ADDITIONAL ARMS	5 x M1 carbine

*Overall dimensions measured with main gun facing forward, and MG mounted.

Production

	1943	1944
January		250
February		218
March		170
April		150
May		150
June		150
July	6	150
August	83	150
September	112	150
October	150	157
November	267	
December	194	

The hull front door has been removed on a late M18, and the transmission and differential assembly has been pulled out of the front of the vehicle using the rails, allowing a view into the driver's and co-driver's compartment. (James Alexander)

In this view, the front hull door has been removed, but the transmission and differential assembly is in place. The differential is the visible part of the assembly; the transmission is out of view aft of the differential. (James Alexander)

The transmission and differential assembly has been pulled partially out of the M18. On the side of the carrier, as the differential housing is called, is the right output shaft, which transfers power to the right final drive. (James Alexander)

The left side of an M18's transmission and differential assembly is displayed. It is a controlled differential, meaning it both transfers power equally to the final drives and also has manually operated brakes within the assembly for steering the vehicle.

The late 76mm GMC M18 in the collection of Steve Preston is observed from overhead, emphasizing the layout of the left side of the vehicle. The design of the turret top is visible, including the .50-caliber machine gun ring mount, the outboard side of which hangs over the left side of the turret. The national symbol, a five-pointed star inside a circle, is applied to the top of the turret bustle, the sides of the hull, and the front of the hull. The circle around the star was introduced in late 1942. This style of star symbol is sometimes called the invasion star. (James Alexander)

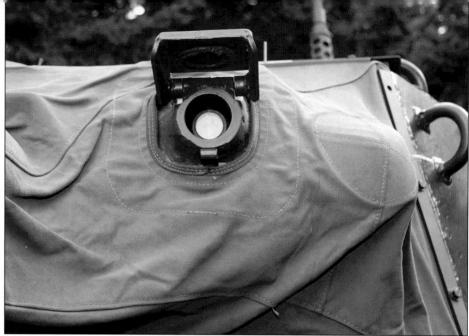

The mantlet cover was sewn from multiple panels of canvas. Steel strips with hex screws hold the top and sides of the cover to the turret, and a webbing strap secures the front of the cover around the barrel. (James Alexander)

With the telescope cover raised, the objective lens of the gunner's telescopic gun sight is visible inside the aperture. The bulge in the canvas mantlet cover to the right provides clearance for the left lifting eye of the mounting plate. (James Alexander)

A numeric placard has been painted on the driver's hatch hood cover bin on the left side of the turret of this late M18. The top of the hood is visible. Toward the top are a lifting eye and several support brackets for the canvas top. (James Alexander)

The same driver's hood and bin shown in the preceding photo is observed from above. Part of the windshield wiper is visible, as are the rods and wing nuts on each side of the frame that are used for securing the hood over the hatch opening. (James Alexander)

To the left is the top of the mantlet cover, aft of which are the gunner's periscope cover and grab rail. Adjacent to the breech and recoil guard of the 76mm gun is the top of the right turret box, on which is mounted a late-type travel lock. Atop the bustle are the antenna mount (mast base unit MP48) and the door for the stowage box. Also in view are the machine gun ring mount, the gunner's and commander's seats, and numerous small details. (James Alexander)

The top of the turret of the late M18 is shown from a slightly different angle. Details worthy of notice include the seatbelt lying on the gunner's seat, the guard around the antenna mount, and the diamond-tread flooring below the turret. (James Alexander)

The door of the stowage box at the rear of the turret bustle is open, as seen from above. A strict schedule of contents of this box was listed in the M18's tech manual. Visible are a collapsible bucket and a canvas cover for the air intake. (James Alexander)

Several bedrolls are secured with webbing straps to the left turret rack. The M18 tech manual, TM 9-755, specified that a 12 x 12 foot tarpaulin and five blanket rolls were to be stowed on the rack on the left side of the turret. (James Alexander)

The bedrolls on the left turret rack are viewed from a different angle. A footman loop is on the bottom of the rack. Underneath the turret on top of the rear deck of the hull, a small portion of the left side of the air intake grille is visible. (James Alexander)

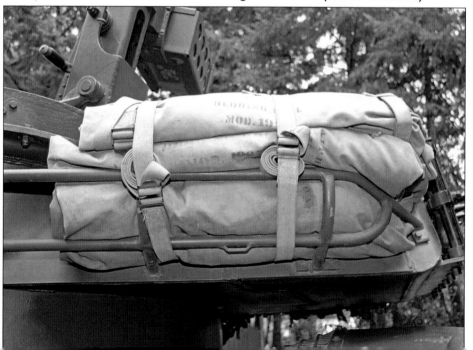

With the .50-caliber machine gun poised above, the left rear corner of the turret of Steve Preston's late-production 76mm GMC M18 is observed, with the left rear corner of the hull, including the left tail light assembly, to the bottom.

Six spare track links are secured in the rack at the rear of the bustle of the M18 turret. Stowage racks flank each side of the turret rear. Visible at the top of the turret is the antenna base.

As illustrated in an overhead view, the 76mm gun and its recoil guard and, in this case, the rail mounted on top of the turret above the gun, bisected the turret from front to rear. The loader's station was to the right of the gun, with the right ammunition box to the front of his station. This box held ready-rounds of 76mm ammunition and boxes of .30-caliber and .50-caliber ammunition. It is apparent how the canted position of the breech aided the loader in inserting ammunition into the breech in the tight confines of the turret. (James Alexander)

A closer view of the turret shows further details, including of the Browning M2 .50-caliber machine gun and its ammunition box. The right turret box is visible in the right side of the turret, including several ready-rounds of 76mm ammunition on the left side of the rack and boxes for machine gun ammunition on the right side of the rack. To the left of the 76mm gun are the gunner's controls for traversing the turret and elevating and firing the gun. A binocular case is on the right side of the turret. (James Alexander)

On the inboard edge of the top of the right turret box is the late-model travel lock for the 76mm gun. The hinge-shaped fixtures on the front edge of the stowage bin on the turret bustle are actually locks, secured with removable pins. (James Alexander)

A rolled camouflage net is stowed in the rack on the right side of the turret bustle. According to the tech manual for the M18, the canvas cover assembly for the turret also was to be stored on this rack when not deployed over the turret. (James Alexander)

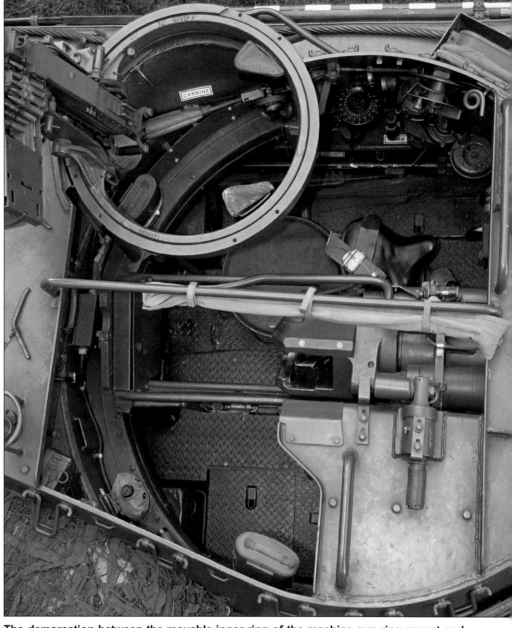

The demarcation between the movable inner ring of the machine gun ring mount and the fixed outer ring of the mount is visible in this overhead view of the Preston M18. The padded cradles on the inner ring, by which the commander/machine gunner pushed the ring around with his upper body, are also in view. An M1 carbine is stowed on the turret wall below the ring mount. Five M1 carbines, one for each crewman, were stowed inside the vehicle. In a box behind the driver's seat was a box for 450 rounds of .30-caliber ammunition for the carbines. (James Alexander)

Another M1 carbine is stored on the right side of the recoil guard of the 76mm gun. A lead weight was added to the rear of the recoil guard of the 76mm gun M1A2, to act as a counterbalance for the weight of the muzzle brake. (James Alexander)

At the center of the forward half of the turret bustle is radio equipment. The top unit with the pull handle is the transmitter-receiver, below which, also with a pull handle, is the plate supply unit. Below the antenna mount is the battery case. (James Alexander)

The mantlet cover of a very late M18 is viewed from the front right corner of the vehicle. It has a russet leather strip at the bottom. Mantlet covers were usually worn, not stored onboard, and were loose fitting to allow for movement of the gun.

In this view of the turret of a late M18, a breech cover has been installed. It fits over not only the 76mm gun's breech but also the recoil guard. To the lower right is a signal flag set M238. On the rail over the turret is a bag for a three-section radio antenna.

This is the late-type travel lock, installed beginning with M18 serial number 1858. The arm is shown swung down in the locked position. A ball stud on the lock was secured in a ball-retainer clamp on the gun's recoil cylinder, to lock the gun in place.

The travel lock on a very late M18 is shown in a partially raised position. To the right of the main bracket of the travel lock is the parking bracket. Visible at the bottom center, on top of the recoil cylinder of the gun, is the ball-retainer clamp.

The same travel lock shown in the preceding image, on Allan Cors's late M18, is shown in the unlocked position. The bottom part of the locking arm is latched to the parking bracket. The coil spring acted to raise the arm when unlocked.

The right turret box to the front of the loader's position in the turret has space for nine rounds of 76mm ammunition on the left and cubbyholes for five boxes of .50-caliber ammunition and one box of .30-caliber ammunition. A binocular case is to the right.

A full view of the right turret box is shown. To keep the ammunition boxes from sliding out of the four lower cubbyholes, a simple but effective circular stop is employed, with a quarter-round cutout to allow one box at a time to be pulled out. Visible beneath the ammo rack is a spare telescope and the spotlight, each in their designated positions. Additional 76mm ammunition was stored in racks in the sponsons on each side of the turret, with 18 rounds per side. A total of 45 rounds of 76mm ammunition could be carried onboard. (James Alexander)

The 76mm gun M1A2 and part of the right turret box of a late M18 are viewed from above. Usually, high-explosive, armor-piercing, and smoke rounds were carried. The counterweight at the rear of the recoil guard of the main gun is visible to the lower left. To the right of the counterweight is a canteen. To the top left is the breech of the gun. The breech-operating handle is to the left of the rear of the breech. The M18 turret did not have a turret basket. Steel floor plates with diamond tread are below the turret. (James Alexander)

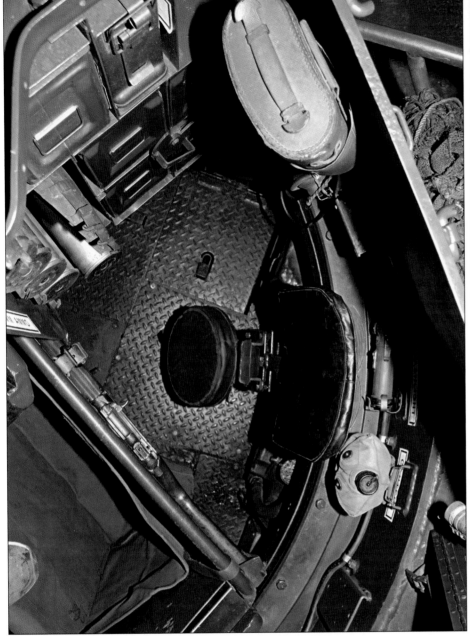

The loader's seat is shown in its service position, in contrast to its stowed position shown in the preceding photo, with the seat lowered. The seat had two height settings using a handle on the right of the seat, and the seat was easily removed. (James Alexander)

The right turret wall is displayed. To the far left is the right turret box, showing the locking wheel, fitted with a handle. Below the binoculars case are an intercom control box and headphones. To the right is a battery case for the radio. (James Alexander)

Looking down into the loader's position to the right of the 76mm gun in a late 76mm GMC M18, the loader's seat back is adjacent to the stowed canteen, and the round seat bottom is in its stowed position. In back of the seat back, a flashlight is in its stowage bracket. To the upper right are binoculars. The M18's on-vehicle equipment listed a set of binoculars M3 in a carrying case M17 on the right side of the turret wall and the left side of the turret wall. To the upper right, the thickness of the turret wall is evident. (James Alexander)

In a view of the right interior of the turret bustle, more of the battery case is visible at the upper center. The loader's seat has been removed from the turret ring adjacent to the flashlight, allowing a partial view of the right air cleaner, below. (James Alexander)

The radio transmitter-receiver (upper box) and the plate supply unit (lower box) of the radio set are attached to a shock-proof mount in the turret bustle. Typically, the SCR 610 radio and the RC99 interphone system were installed in the M18.

Below the canteen is the front of the rear transfer case, which transmits power from the engine to the transmission via the propeller shaft, and provides a means of detaching the engine from the drive train when the engine is removed. (James Alexander)

There is scant clearance between the recoil guard of the 76mm gun and the turret ring. A canvas spent-casing catcher is installed on the rails of the recoil guard. The breech block has been opened, exposing the gun's chamber to view. (James Alexander)

On the left turret wall of the Preston M18 are, left to right, an M1 carbine, the azimuth indicator (center), a flashlight, and the traverse gear box and motor and hand control, above which is a reel with 25 yards of communications wire. (James Alexander)

At the center, on the left side of the turret, is the remote control lever, linked to the traversing mechanism, that allowed the commander to traverse the turret. Pulling back on the lever resulted in a left traverse; pushing it forward caused a right traverse. (Steve Preston)

The left rear of the turret of the M18 is viewed from the gunner's position, with a microphone and headphones to the lower right and the machine gun ring mount at the top. The black box aft of the canteen is the intercom amplifier BC667. (James Alexander)

In this view into the left side of the turret, the 76mm gun is at the top, the spent-casing collector bag is to the right, the rim of the ring mount is to the upper right, and the gunner's seat and commander's seat/platform are at the bottom. (James Alexander)

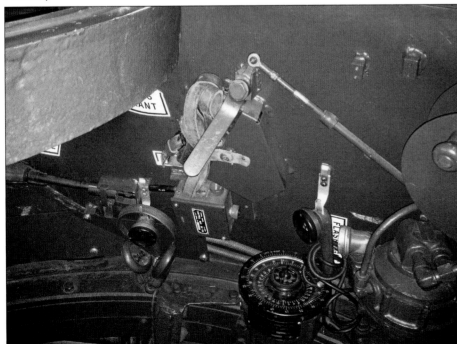

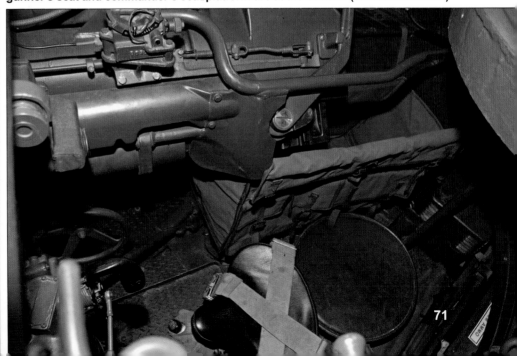

Facing to the left front of the fighting compartment below the turret, at the center is the slip ring. Electrical current to power turret components is transmitted from the ring through cables in the drag link to the right of the slip ring. (James Alexander)

Shown close-up, left to right, are the azimuth indicator, traverse gear box and motor, manual traverse control handle, and, mounted on the turret ring, the turret lock. Turning the handle on the turret lock rearward locked the turret in place. (James Alexander)

Seen from behind the gunner's seat in the Preston late M18, stowed 76mm ammunition is to the left, the 76mm gun breech and its operating handle are to the right, and the electro-hydraulic traversing mechanism is to the front of the seat. (James Alexander)

The same elements shown in the preceding photo are observed from above. In addition, to the right is the electro-hydraulic traverse mechanism, comprising an electric motor on the bottom, and a hand control and hydraulic pump on top.

This view illustrates the gunner's controls. The hand traverse control, left of center, was used in the event of failure of the electro-hydraulic traverse mechanism, at the center. To the right is the hand wheel for controlling the elevation of the gun. (James Alexander)

The gunner's telescope for direct laying of the 76mm gun has a rubber eyepiece and an illuminated reticle for night firing. M72C and M76C telescopes were used on the M18s, placed on the telescope mount M55. The lever with the ball end is the hand firing lever for the main gun.

This is how the gunner saw his "office" from his seat. At the lower center is the black hand control for the electro-hydraulic traverse. Above that control is the periscope. To the upper right of the control are the telescopic gun sight and firing lever. (James Alexander)

This is the electro-hydraulic traverse mechanism in a very late M18. The handle actually controlled the hydraulic pump; turning the handle to the left traversed the turret to the left, and vice-versa. To the right is the elevating hand wheel.

To the right of the traverse motor (left) is the electro-hydraulic traverse switch panel. Normally, the 76mm gun was fired using the electric foot switch on the floor at the lower left. The hand firing lever was used in the event this electric switch failed.

The elevation quadrant has a spirit level on top. The curved, black scale is the elevation coarse scale, in 100-mil intervals. At the rear are the elevating knob and the micrometer, set at 1-mil intervals. The quadrant had lamps for use at night. (James Alexander)

As viewed from the left side of the turret of a late-production M18, mounted atop the gun at the upper center of the photograph is the elevation quadrant M9. This instrument was used to lay the elevation of the gun when conducting indirect-fire missions. To the right of the elevation quadrant at the top of the photo is the recoil cylinder. Also in view is the eyepiece and crash pad of the telescope, the elevating hand wheel, and the hand control for the electro-hydraulic traverse. The twisted object at the bottom left is the guide ring for the communications cable stored on a reel next to it. (James Alexander)

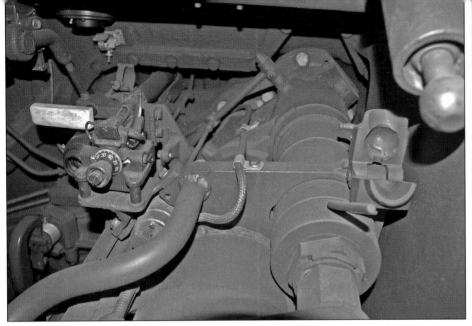

The elevation quadrant M9 is viewed from the rear. An elevation scale is also on the right side of the instrument. To the top right is the ball stud of the travel lock, with the ball-retainer clamp and release handle below it atop the recoil cylinder of the 76mm gun.

The breechblock-operating handle is connected by a roller chain to the closing spring (lower left). After manually opening the breechblock, further operation of the breech was automatic until the last round was fired. (James Alexander)

The Honeywell gunner's quadrant M1 is mounted on top of the 76mm gun breech. This detachable instrument was used for measuring the elevation or depression of the gun and served as a backup for the elevation quadrant M9. (Steve Preston)

To set the gun at a desired elevation, the scales on the quadrant were set, and the gun was elevated until the bubble in the spirit level was centered. When not in use, the quadrant was stored in a case on the turret's left wall. (James Alexander)

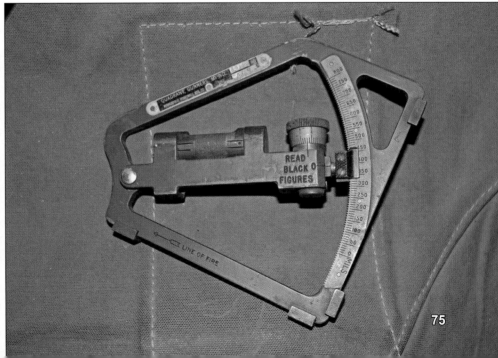

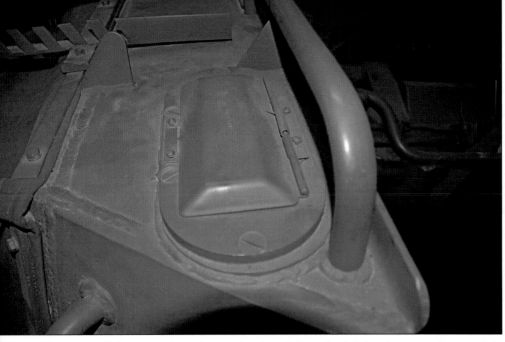

The cover of the gunner's periscope is viewed from the left front corner of a very late M18. The cover is hinged at the rear, and coil springs on the hinge act to hold the cover down when the periscope is lowered. The gunner's vane sites are also in view.

It is speculated that this fixture bolted to the top front of the turret of the very late M18 is a device for lashing the parking brakes "on" during transport, permitting the brakes to be released without entering the vehicle. Also in view is the .50-caliber gun barrel.

A half-century after World War II, a few M18s continued to serve with the Serbian Army, including this example assigned to the 7th Brigade. It featured a colorful camouflage scheme simulating foliage, with what appears to have been light green, yellowish green, and black leaves over a base coat of Olive Green.

7BRIGADA
SUADALIL^C

The driver's compartment is seen through the open hatch, showing the transmission housing, the seat, a container for periscope spare heads to the right, and the guard for the final-drive universal joint to the left. A weatherproof gasket surrounds the hatch.

Behind the driver's seat to the lower left is the master switch box, with two switches for controlling the 12-volt and 24-volt currents. The red cap on top of the box protects a receptacle for connecting an outside or slave battery to the vehicle. (James Alexander)

The driver's station is viewed from the co-driver's station in a late M18, with a periscope box and the instrument panel in the sponson in the background. To the right are the driver's hand levers for controlling the steering. (James Alexander)

The driver's steering levers (but not the co-driver's) are toothed quadrants with locking pawls, allowing the steering controls to be used as parking-brake controls. To engage the parking brakes, both levers were pulled back and locked. (James Alexander)

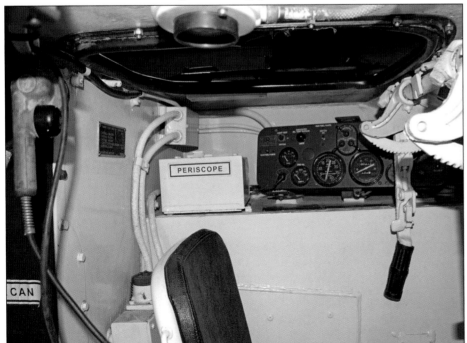

Below the guard for the final-drive universal joint is the driver's accelerator pedal, made of steel mesh. On the U-shaped bracket between the steering levers is the compass. The black knob to the far right is for adjusting the steering brakes. (James Alexander)

On the top left side of the transmission housing is the transmission manual shift lever and bracket. It provided for five gear settings: neutral, reverse, and three forward gears. Marked on the bracket are the speed ranges for each forward gear. (James Alexander)

The co-driver's hatch doors on a late M18 are open, permitting a glimpse into the compartment below. The cross-shaft of the co-driver's steering system is near the front edge of the hatch. Technical manuals are arrayed on the co-driver's seat.

In the co-driver's compartment, to the upper left a link from the steering controls is fastened to the right control lever of the differential. Two headlights are stowed above the universal joint guard, to the right of which is a decontamination kit. (James Alexander)

In the right sponson next to the co-driver's seat are a portable fire extinguisher and a five-gallon fuel tank for the auxiliary generator. To the lower right are the interior control handles and their guard for the fixed fire-extinguisher system. (James Alexander)

Behind the co-driver's seat is the Homelite auxiliary generator. It was powered by a gasoline motor and was used to charge the vehicle's batteries when the engine generator was not working, as well as to supplement the engine generator. (James Alexander)

The interior control handles for the fixed fire-extinguisher system are viewed from another angle, with the co-driver's seatback to the right. Pulling these handles activated carbon-dioxide cylinders to put out fires in the engine compartment. (James Alexander)

The Homelite HRUH-28 auxiliary generator, sometimes nicknamed the "Little Joe," is viewed from a different angle. It was rated at 1,500 watts, 30 volts a.c. The auxiliary generator engine was a single-cylinder, air-cooled, two-cycle design.

More than a half-century after production ceased on the 76mm GMC M18, a surviving example shows how it can still tear up the turf on an off-road course. The M18 suffered from developmental problems and had several inherent weaknesses, such as thin armor, an open-topped turret that left its crew exposed to enemy snipers and artillery, and a main gun that was ill-equipped to cope with the German Panther and Tiger tanks. As the war progressed, the M18 was increasingly diverted from its antitank role to infantry-support missions. Nevertheless, the vehicle compiled a worthy record as a key part of the U.S. Army's Tank Destroyer Force in World War II.